Editor in Chief
Ina Massler Levin, M.A.

Editor
Eric Migliaccio

Contributing Editor
Sarah Smith

Creative Director
Karen J. Goldfluss, M.S. Ed.

Cover Design
Tony Carrillo / Marilyn Goldberg

Teacher Created Resources
12621 Western Avenue
Garden Grove, CA 92841
www.teachercreated.com

ISBN: 978-1-4206-5925-2

Reprinted, 2025 (PO605846)
Made in U.S.A.

Teacher Created Resources

This book belongs to

____

Ready·Set·Learn

Get Ready to Learn!

Get ready, get set, and go! Boost your child's learning with this exciting series of books. Geared to help children practice and master many needed skills, the *Ready·Set·Learn* books are bursting with 64 pages of learning fun. Use these books for . . .

- enrichment
- skills reinforcement
- extra practice

With their smaller size, the *Ready·Set·Learn* books fit easily in children's hands, backpacks, and book bags. All your child needs to get started are pencils, crayons, and colored pencils.

A full sheet of colorful stickers is included. Use these stickers for . . .

- decorating pages
- rewarding outstanding effort
- keeping track of completed pages

Celebrate your child's progress by using these stickers on the reward chart located on the inside cover. The blue-ribbon sticker fits perfectly on the certificate on page 64.

With *Ready·Set·Learn* and a little encouragement, your child will be on the fast track to learning fun!

Practicing A to L

Directions: Practice your cursive writing. Copy the letters on the lines.

Aa Bb Cc Dd

Ee Ff Gg Hh

Ii Jj Kk Ll

Practicing M to Z

Directions: Practice your cursive writing. Copy the letters on the lines.

Mm Nn Oo Pp

Qq Rr Ss Tt

Uu Vv Ww Xx

Yy Zz

Puppies!

Directions: Look at the picture and the words around it. Use cursive to write two sentences about the picture. Use as many of the words as possible. Add other words to complete your sentences.

Ending in Y

Directions: Write the plural forms of the nouns below.

1. penny
2. pony
3. berry
4. family
5. factory
6. candy
7. party
8. cherry
9. baby
10. belly
11. jelly
12. lily
13. lady
14. patty
15. fly
16. story

Just Add an SSSSS

Directions: Change each noun to a plural noun by adding the letter *s*. Write the new word on the line provided.

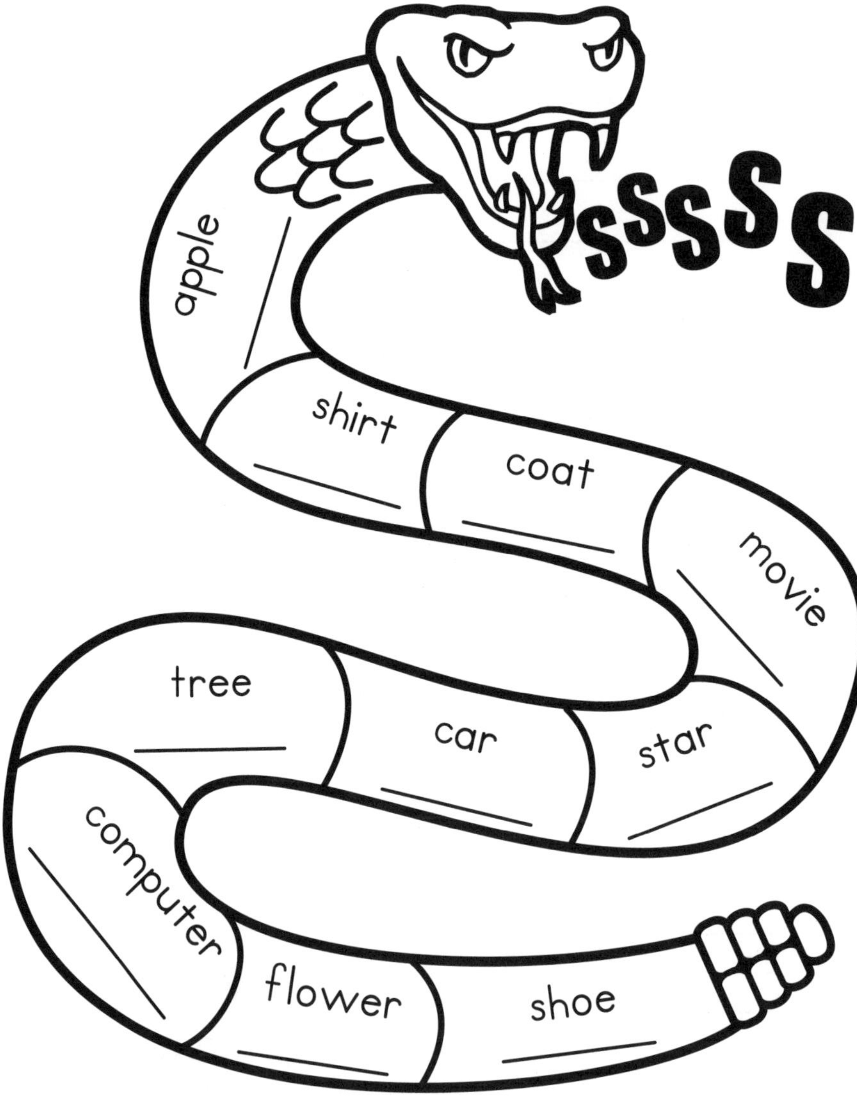

Pronoun Match

Directions: Draw lines to match the pronouns on the left with the nouns on the right.

Pronouns	Nouns
he	sunshine
she	Mandy
it	Brett, Sadie, and Phil
we	Joan and I
they	Jack

Capital Check

Directions: Circle the capitalization errors in each sentence. Then write each sentence correctly.

1. i like to pretend that i can travel through time.

2. once i pretended to visit a king and queen.

3. they took me to their castle, where i met a dragon.

4. the dragon was friendly, so i named him norbert.

5. norbert and i flew around the kingdom in the sky.

Comprehension Check

Directions: Read the story and answer the questions below.

Cowboys

Cowboys can be found living and working throughout the world. In Italy, cowboys are called "butteros." In Argentina, they are known as "gauchos." In Spain, they are called "vaqueros."

A cowboy's hat is his trademark. The hats reflect regional differences but are used in much the same way. The hat is used to shade the cowboy's eyes and to protect him from the sun. When it rains, the hat is used like an umbrella. The hat can be used to carry water and to fan the flames of the campfire. The hat also protects the cowboy's head from low-hanging tree branches and thorny shrubs.

1. What are cowboys called in other parts of the world?

2. Write at least two uses for the cowboy's hat.

What Kind of Noun?

Directions: Complete each sentence with the kind of noun written before the sentence.

person	**1.**	The ____________________ delivered the mail.
thing	**2.**	I cannot find my ________________________.
thing	**3.**	The dog played with the __________________.
person	**4.**	Jeff and ____________ played ball in the park.
place	**5.**	I read my book at the ___________________.
person	**6.**	________________________ played the piano.
place	**7.**	Can we go to the _______________________?
thing	**8.**	At the store, I bought ___________________.
person	**9.**	_________________ and I saw a movie today.
thing	**10.**	Phil ate _______________________ for lunch.

Action Verbs

Directions: Underline the action verbs in the following sentences. The first one has been done for you.

1. Marie enjoys running.
2. She runs with a group of people every Sunday.
3. One person marks a four-mile trail with flour.
4. The rest of them search for the trail.
5. The runners splash through puddles and leap over fallen logs.
6. They climb over fences and fall in the mud.
7. Finally, they burst across the finish line.
8. Marie and her friends wash their hands and faces.
9. Then they sit in the park and drink water.
10. Later, they eat spaghetti and talk about how much fun they had that day.

Which Verb?

Directions: Circle the correct verb for each sentence.

1.	We ________ the book.	**read**	**reads**
2.	We ________ the circus.	**watch**	**watches**
3.	Mr. Kim ________ across the pool.	**swim**	**swims**
4.	Her dog Lucky ________ cats.	**chase**	**chases**
5.	The panda ________ the tree.	**climb**	**climbs**
6.	I ________ a mile.	**run**	**runs**
7.	You ________ up the mountain.	**hike**	**hikes**
8.	They ________ to 100.	**count**	**counts**
9.	She ________ the violin.	**play**	**plays**
10.	They ________ the kite.	**fly**	**flies**

Past or Present

Directions: Each present contains two verbs. Circle the verb that is present tense. Draw a square around the verb that is past tense.

1. finish / finished
2. carry / carried
3. cleaned / clean
4. painted / paint
5. walk / walked
6. laughed / laugh
7. lifted / lift
8. grinned / grin
9. wrap / wrapped

Animal Adjectives

Directions: Adjectives are used to describe nouns. Adjectives tell which one, what kind, and how many. Read each story. Add the missing adjectives.

475	hard	many	slow-moving

The Turtle

The ______________ turtle has a ______________ shell. The turtle can live for ______________ years. The heaviest turtle can weigh ______________ pounds!

good	sharp	long	tree-living

The Chameleon

A chameleon is a ______________ lizard. It has ______________ claws on its toes and ______________ eyesight. The chameleon also has a ______________ tongue that it uses to catch insects.

Two into One

Directions: Draw a line and match each set of words to the correct contraction.

1. does not	**a.** weren't
2. will not	**b.** aren't
3. has not	**c.** hadn't
4. was not	**d.** doesn't
5. is not	**e.** Jack's
6. did not	**f.** hasn't
7. had not	**g.** wasn't
8. were not	**h.** isn't
9. are not	**i.** didn't
10. Jack is	**j.** won't

Punctuation Practice

Directions: Add a period (**.**), a question mark (**?**), or an exclamation point (**!**) to the end of each sentence.

1. He can go with him ☐

2. Where are you ☐

3. Help ☐

4. Who made the bed ☐

5. Go to third base ☐

6. I like to eat cookies ☐

7. What a fine job ☐

8. The tools are in the shed ☐

9. How much do you want ☐

10. What is your name ☐

Comma Time

Directions: Add the commas where they belong.

1. Yes I would love to go to the movie.
2. We have potato chips cheese and chili.
3. Grandma could we please spend the night?
4. This red car belongs to my mom and this blue car belongs to my dad.
5. John may I borrow your football?
6. We saw swans ducks and an ostrich.
7. Invite Casey Jackie and Toby to go with us.
8. No we can't go to the zoo today.
9. My sister likes hot dogs and I like pizza.
10. Aunt Irene my mom's sister liked the book but I liked the movie.

Sentence Scramble

Directions: Unscramble the words to make sentences. Be sure to add a capital letter at the beginning and punctuation at the end of each sentence.

1. bird cat the chased the

2. letter friend I a wrote my to

3. puzzle the made a family

4. sea jumped into penguin a the

5. song to a puppets audience the sang the

About Barn Owls

Directions: Read the paragraph below. Color the owl that has the main idea.

Barn owls are fully grown by about 12 weeks of age. First, they hatch from eggs. At three weeks, their eyes are open, and they can jump and walk. Three weeks later, their feathers begin to grow. By eight weeks, they are practicing flight and are ready to leave their nests. Two weeks later, they begin to explore on their own. Finally, by 12 weeks they are grown and can hunt for food on their own.

Alphabetical Order

Directions: List these words in alphabetical order.

river	house	silent
moon	ghost	tunnel
friend	vest	jump

Directions: List these words in alphabetical order. You will need to look at the second letters, as well as the first.

dog	lunch	science
sort	cane	cell
loop	lion	deer

Practicing Sequence

Directions: Number the pictures in order. Color the pictures.

Practicing Analogies

Directions: Read the words that are being compared. Fill in each blank with the best word from the word box.

bird	goal	night	skin	winter
coloring	head	quack	swim	year

1. *Chicken* is to *cluck* as *duck* is to ______________________.

2. *Banana* is to *peel* as *apple* is to ______________________.

3. *Football* is to *touchdown* as *hockey* is to ________________.

4. *Bird* is to *fly* as *fish* is to ____________________________.

5. *Leaf* is to *tree* as *feather* is to _______________________.

6. *Pencil* is to *writing* as *crayon* is to __________________.

7. *Light* is to *day* as *dark* is to __________________________.

8. *Day* is to *week* as *month* is to ________________________.

9. *Hot* is to *summer* as *cold* is to _______________________.

10. *Roof* is to *house* as *hat* is to ________________________.

Synonym Practice

Directions: Synonyms are two or more words that have similar meanings. Read each clue, look at the list in the box below, and complete the crossword puzzle.

Across

2. difficult
4. rear
6. all
8. help
9. end

Down

1. large
3. old
5. sudden
7. dark

abrupt	**back**	**every**
ancient	**dim**	**hard**
assist	**enormous**	**stop**

Correct It

Directions: Rewrite each sentence. Insert quotation marks, commas, periods, question marks, and exclamation points to punctuate each sentence. Capitalize letters wherever needed.

1. I have a dog named butch who likes to dig roll and play fetch.

____

____

2. marvin t adams rode his bike to school on september 4 2007

____

____

3. i like the poem the homework machine by shel silverstein

____

____

4. there is a tall gnarly tree on hiss st in gainstown illinois

____

____

5. while looking out the window, sheila shouted look out

____

____

Proofreading Practice

Directions: Proofreading means reading a story or sentences and finding and correcting the mistakes. Read the story and circle the 9 mistakes. Write the circled words correctly on the lines below.

A Stinky Jog

my dad loves to jogg! Every nite after work, my dad puts on his tennis shues and hits the pavement.
usually, nothing exciting or smelly ever happins. But one night, as it was getting dark, my dad smelled a horrible odor coming from the bushes! My dad jogged over to the bushes and pulled the branchs aside. Can you guess what happened next. There was a skunck hiding in the bushes, and it sprayed my dad!

____________ ____________ ____________

____________ ____________ ____________

____________ ____________ ____________

Simon Says

Directions: In the game Simon Says, everyone has to obey Simon's commands. Read each sentence. If the sentence is a command, write the letter **C** on the line. If not, write **N**.

_______ **1.** Go to the office.

_______ **2.** What a beautiful ring!

_______ **3.** Sit next to me.

_______ **4.** Answer the phone.

_______ **5.** Do you know my name?

_______ **6.** Give me more dessert.

_______ **7.** That pie is delicious.

_______ **8.** Get ready to go.

_______ **9.** I love you.

_______ **10.** Answer the next question.

Quotation Marks

Directions: Read each quote and add quotation marks wherever they are needed.

1. I can't wait for summer vacation, Ted said.

2. I can't wait, either, Addison agreed.

3. Where are you going on vacation? Ted asked.

4. We're going to Hawaii, Addison said.

5. That sounds very nice, Ted replied.

6. Where are you going? Addison asked.

7. Ted replied, Well, it's not exactly Hawaii, but there is water there.

8. Well, where is it? Addison asked again.

9. I'm going to spend my vacation working at my Uncle Bob's carwash, Ted finally told her.

10. I guess you're right, Addison said with a smile. There will be plenty of water.

Something Different

Directions: Write the plural form of each noun.

1. goose ______________________________

2. story ______________________________

3. man ______________________________

4. ox ______________________________

5. leaf ______________________________

6. berry ______________________________

7. lady ______________________________

8. deer ______________________________

9. penny ______________________________

10. woman ______________________________

Proper and Common

Directions: Read each sentence. Draw a circle around any proper nouns. Place an **X** on any common nouns.

1. Jennifer always gets pizza for supper on Fridays.

2. My friend is a nice person.

3. Can you and Joe bake the cake?

4. Mom and Dad are going to the game.

5. Chloe and Kayla Beth are sisters.

6. The bus took the students to school.

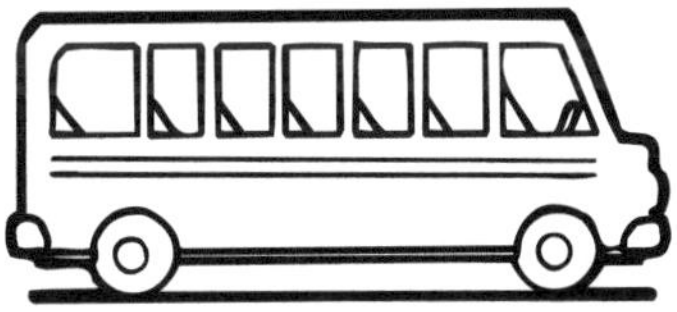

7. Ella gave the teacher an apple.

8. Gage gave the teacher a pencil.

9. Sally saw a huge snake in the tree.

10. The day was Tuesday.

Describe It

Directions: List two adjectives that can describe each noun.

Example: apple ___red___ and ___shiny___

1. boy __________ and __________

2. girl __________ and __________

3. school __________ and __________

4. dog __________ and __________

5. home __________ and __________

6. summer __________ and __________

7. cars __________ and __________

8. sports __________ and __________

9. pizza __________ and __________

10. flowers __________ and __________

GREAT
#1
YEAH!
COOL
WOW
NEAT
NEAT
GREAT
YEAH!
#1
GREAT
SUPER
WOW
YEAH!
#1
TOPS
SUPER
#1

#1
GREAT
YEAH!
WOW
GREAT
YEAH!
WOW
COOL
YEAH!
TOPS
TOPS
SUPER

Playing Genie

Directions: Imagine you are a genie in a bottle and instead of giving out just the standard three wishes, you can grant 10 wishes to anyone you want. Make the following kids' wishes come true by writing and using an apostrophe to give them what they want.

Example: Joe wants a skateboard. Joe's skateboard

1. Emily wants some candy. ______
2. Chien wants a DVD. ______
3. Tyrese wants a new backpack. ______
4. Rafael wants a camera. ______
5. Keysha wants a necklace. ______
6. Elissa wants a game. ______
7. Sharon wants a puzzle. ______
8. Samuel wants some shoes. ______
9. Aina wants a book. ______
10. Brody wants a bike. ______

Practice with Ordinals

Directions: Follow the directions to answer each question.

1. Circle the 2nd bee.

Draw a line under the 4th bee.

2. Circle the 3rd umbrella.

Draw a line under the 1st umbrella.

3. Circle the 4th dragon.

Draw a line under the 6th dragon.

4. Which animal is 1st in line?

5. Which animal is 3rd in line?

Number Sense

Directions: Follow the directions to complete the patterns in each box.

1. Complete the pattern.

2, 4, 6, ___, ___, ___, ___, ___, ___, ___, ___, ___, ___

2. Complete the pattern.

3, 6, 9, ___, ___, ___, ___, ___, ___, ___, ___, ___, ___

3. Complete the pattern.

4, 8, 12, ___, ___, ___, ___, ___, ___, ___, ___, ___, ___

4. Complete the pattern.

	+ 7	**– 4**	**+ 8**	**– 3**	**+ 4**
5					

5. Complete the pattern.

	+ 2	**– 5**	**+ 6**	**– 4**	**+ 7**
9					

Number Words

Directions: Write each number next to its number word. Then use the number words to complete the crossword puzzle below.

eighty ______	hundred ______	ten ______
fifty ______	ninety ______	thirty ______
forty ______	sixty ______	twenty ______

Across

1. 60 + 20
4. 100 – 10
8. 10 + 10
9. 20 + 10

Down

2. 50 + 50
3. 60 – 10
5. 0 + 10
6. 30 + 30
7. 20 + 20

Ready · Set · Learn

Word Problems

Directions: Solve each word problem. Show your work.

1. Jason invited 39 girls and 22 boys to his party. How many children did Jason invite in all? __61__ children were invited.	$\begin{array}{r} 39 \\ +22 \\ \hline 61 \end{array}$
2. Mariah bought 152 balloons, 127 party hats, and 213 candles for the party. How many party items did Mariah buy in all? Mariah bought ________ items.	
3. Beau sent out 185 invitations. 87 people said "yes." The rest said "no." How many people said "no"? ________ people said "no."	
4. Lucy set out 210 green jellybeans and 112 blue jellybeans.. How many jellybeans did Lucy set out in all? Lucy set out ________ jellybeans.	
5. We put sprinkles on 3 cupcakes. We used 567 sprinkles in all. The first cupcake had 237 sprinkles. The second had 197. How many sprinkles did the third cupcake have? It ________ sprinkles.	

Now write the answers in order from smallest to greatest.

__________, __________, __________, __________, __________

Take Away

Directions: Subtract to find the answer.

1. $\begin{array}{r} 55 \\ -\ 22 \\ \hline \end{array}$	**2.** $\begin{array}{r} 98 \\ -\ 43 \\ \hline \end{array}$	**3.** $\begin{array}{r} 43 \\ -\ 12 \\ \hline \end{array}$
4. $\begin{array}{r} 76 \\ -\ 45 \\ \hline \end{array}$	**5.** $\begin{array}{r} 78 \\ -\ 20 \\ \hline \end{array}$	**6.** $\begin{array}{r} 44 \\ -\ 17 \\ \hline \end{array}$
7. $\begin{array}{r} 85 \\ -\ 40 \\ \hline \end{array}$	**8.** $\begin{array}{r} 30 \\ -\ 15 \\ \hline \end{array}$	**9.** $\begin{array}{r} 21 \\ -\ 11 \\ \hline \end{array}$
10. $\begin{array}{r} 66 \\ -\ 33 \\ \hline \end{array}$	**11.** $\begin{array}{r} 12 \\ -\ 2 \\ \hline \end{array}$	**12.** $\begin{array}{r} 90 \\ -\ 45 \\ \hline \end{array}$

Going Down

Directions: Add the columns to find the correct answers.

1. 8 14 + 45	**2.** 12 66 + 21	**3.** 17 81 + 13
4. 48 17 + 22	**5.** 52 37 + 6	**6.** 90 8 + 12

Directions: Add to find the answers.

7. 7 + 23 + 18 = ______

8. 87 + 10 + 5 = ______

9. 20 + 30 + 40 = ______

10. 51 + 60 + 3 = ______

11. 33 + 33 + 33 = ______

12. 84 + 2 + 10 = ______

Practice, Practice, Practice

Directions: Subtract to find the correct answers.

1. 431 − 219	**2.** 786 − 354	**3.** 871 − 44
4. 761 − 321	**5.** 647 − 456	**6.** 321 − 201
7. 987 − 625	**8.** 651 − 412	**9.** 777 − 563
10. 679 − 324	**11.** 411 − 346	**12.** 983 − 890
13. 781 − 708	**14.** 677 − 667	**15.** 156 − 121

Math with Decimals

Directions: Solve each math problem.

1. 93.82 + 60.11	**2.** 14.86 + 84.02	**3.** 24.37 + 54.32
4. 37.58 + 52.30	**5.** 68.46 + 17.02	**6.** 57.32 + 34.00

Directions: Read and solve each world problem. Show your work.

7. Jessica went shopping. She spent $14.10 buying a shirt and $23.67 buying a pair of shoes. How much money did Jessica spend in all?

____

8. Tyrone had $38.59 in his piggy bank. He spent $25.06 buying a video game. How much money does Tyrone have left?

____

Hand in Hand

Directions: Adding and multiplying go hand in hand. Complete each pair of number sentences.

1. 4 + 4 + 4 + 4 = 16   4 x 4 = 16

2. 5 + 5 + 5 + 5 + 5 =   5 x 5 =

3. 6 + 6 + 6 =   6 x 3 =

4. 2 + 2 + 2 + 2 + 2 + 2 =   2 x 6 =

5. 8 + 8 =   8 x 2 =

6. 7 + 7 + 7 + 7 =   7 x 4 =

Multiplication Balloon

Directions: Complete the number sentences. Color the picture using the key. Check your answers using a calculator.

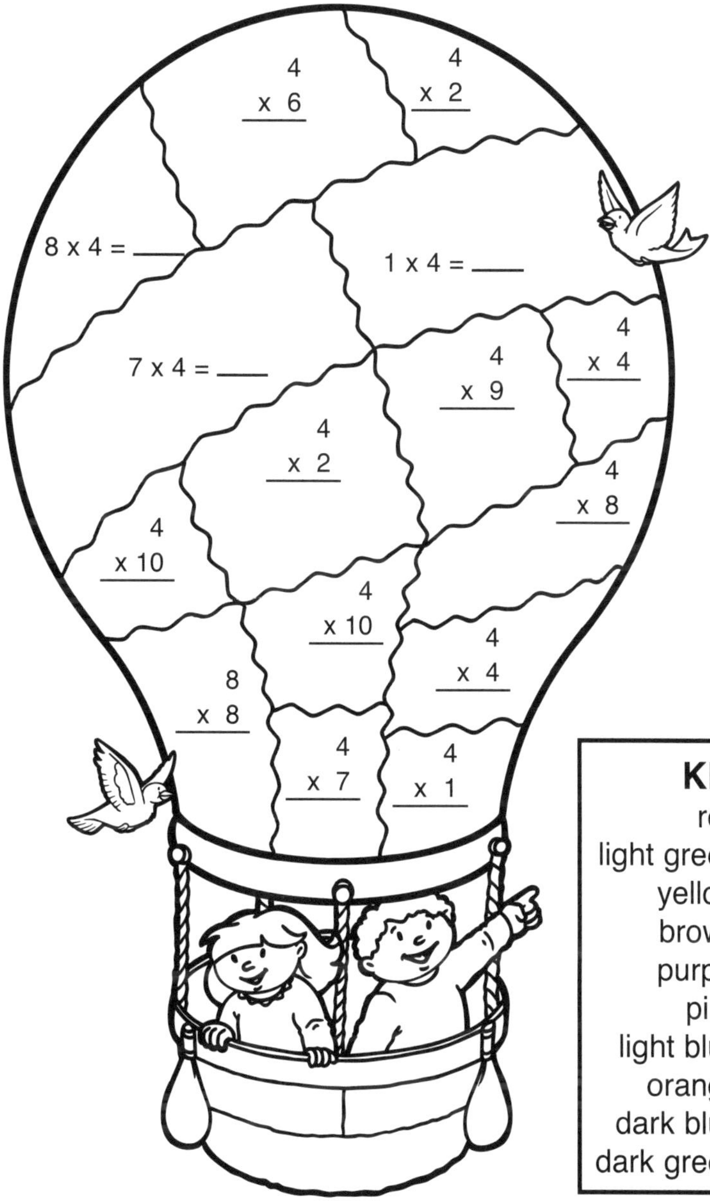

KEY

red = 4
light green = 8
yellow = 16
brown = 20
purple = 24
pink = 28
light blue = 32
orange = 36
dark blue = 40
dark green = 64

Beginning Division

Directions: Divide each set into two equal groups by drawing a box around each group. If there is a remainder, circle the remainder.

1.

2.

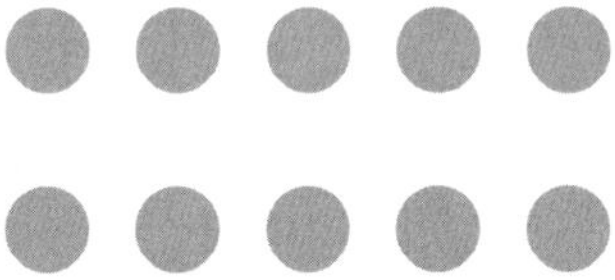

3.

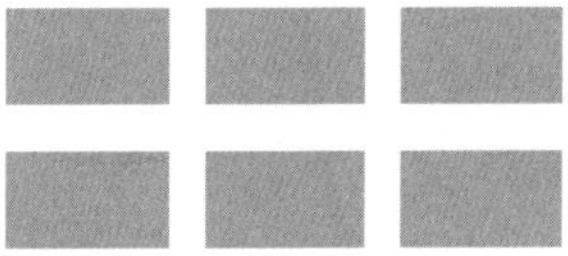

4.

5.

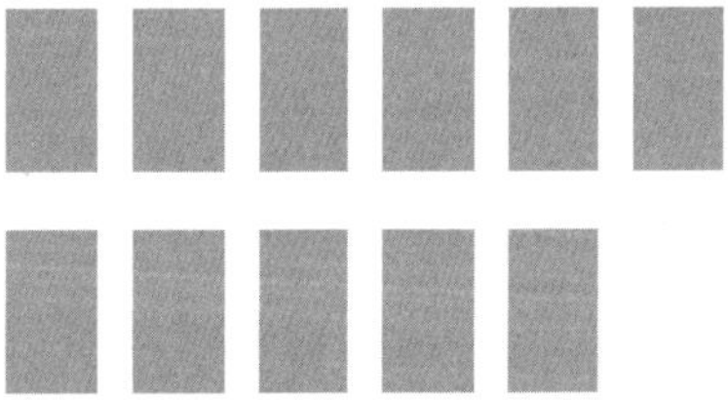

6.

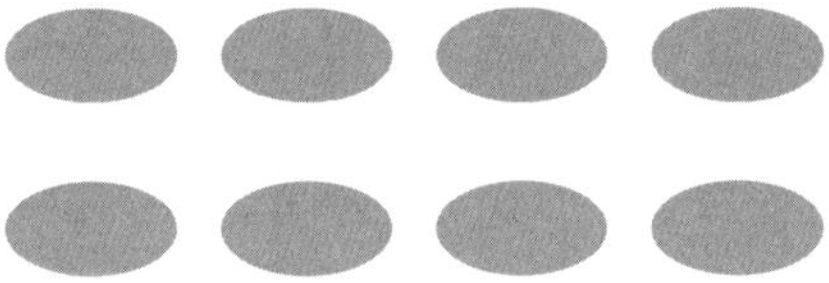

7.

8.

? ? ? ? ?

? ? ? ?

? ? ? ?

Solve the Riddle

Directions: Solve each division problem to find the hidden sentence below.

1. 21 ÷ 7 = ______ **O**

2. 16 ÷ 8 = ______ **R**

3. 81 ÷ 9 = ______ **Y**

4. 40 ÷ 8 = ______ **U**

5. 56 ÷ 8 = ______ **M**

6. 108 ÷ 9 = _____ **S**

7. 7 ÷ 7 = _______ **A**

8. 32 ÷ 8 = ______ **A**

9. 99 ÷ 9 = ______ **T**

10. 42 ÷ 7 = ______ **E**

11. 72 ÷ 9 = ______ **R**

___	___	___		___	___	___		___	___	___	___	___!
9	3	5		1	2	6		12	7	4	8	11

Money! Money! Money!

Directions: Count to find each value. Write the answer on the line.

1.  = ________

2.  = ________

3.  = ________

4.  = ________

5.  = ________

6.  = ________

7.  = ________

8.  = ________

Everywhere Area

Area is the number of square units in a particular space. To find the area of a shape, count the number of squares. The area for this figure is 11 square units.

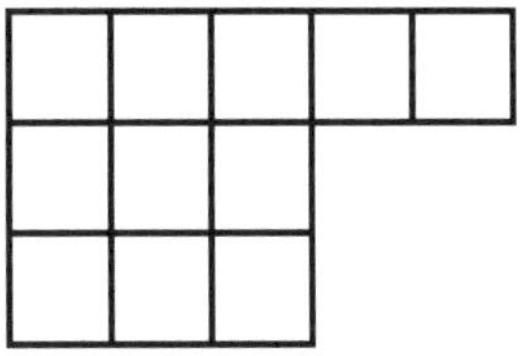

1. ______________ square units

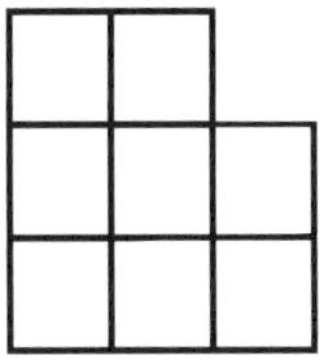

2. ______________ square units

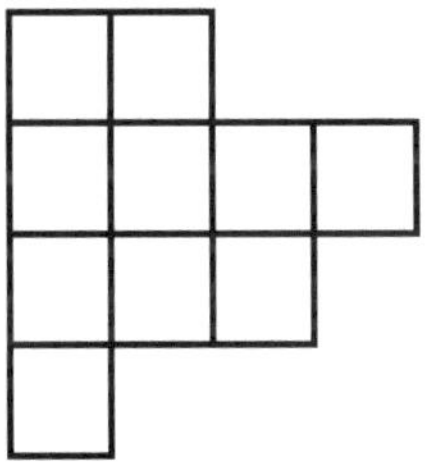

3. ______________ square units

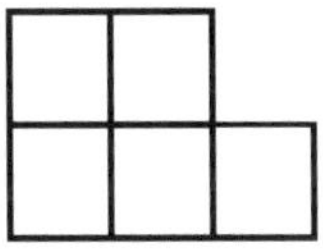

4. ______________ square units

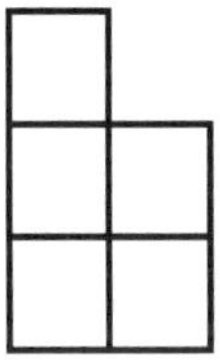

5. ______________ square units

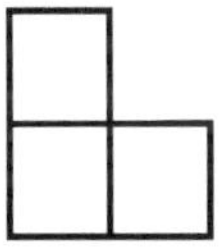

6. ______________ square units

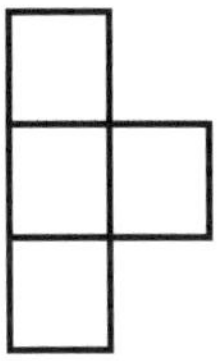

To the right, draw a figure that has 8 square units.

Picture Fraction

Directions: Write a fraction for the shaded part of each picture.

1.

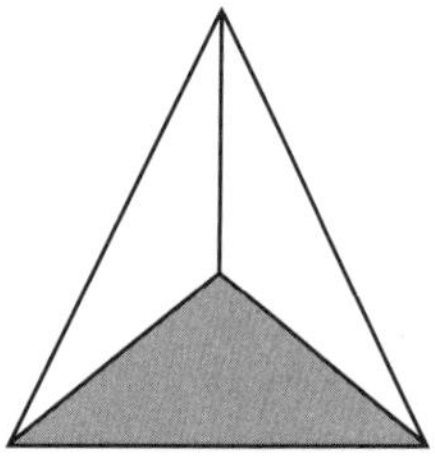

____

2.

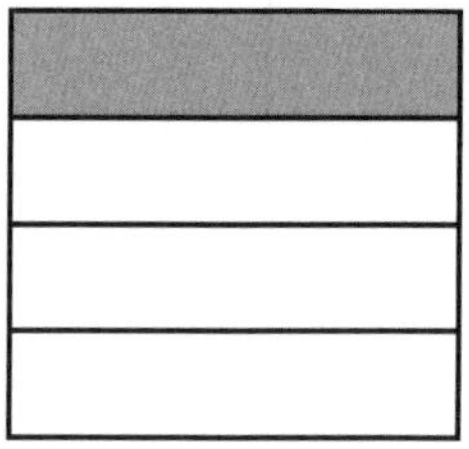

____

3.

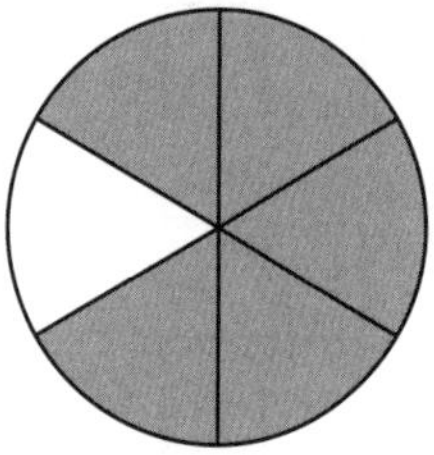

____

4.

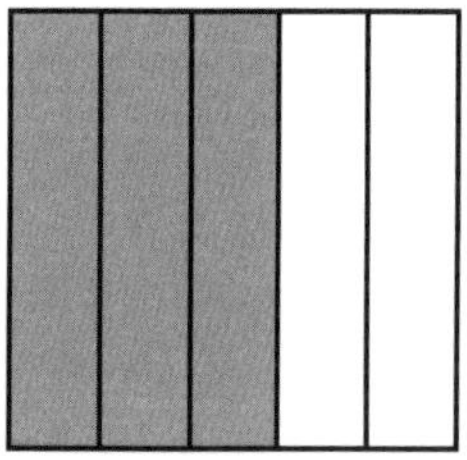

____

5.

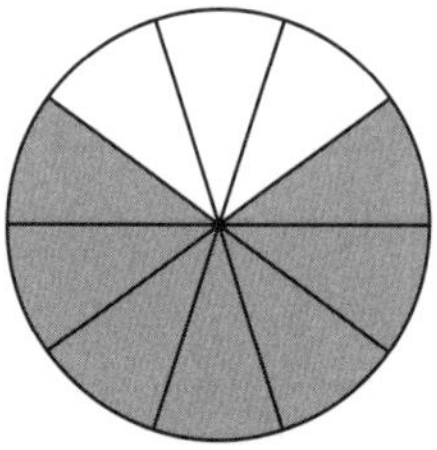

____

6.

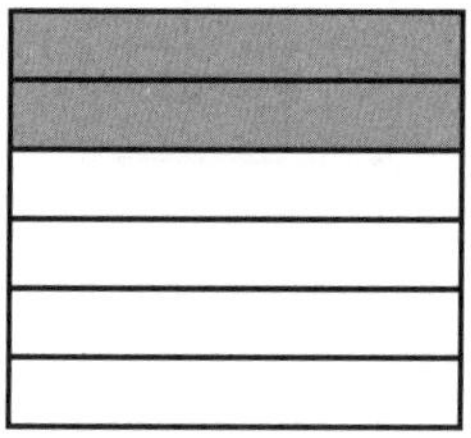

____

7.

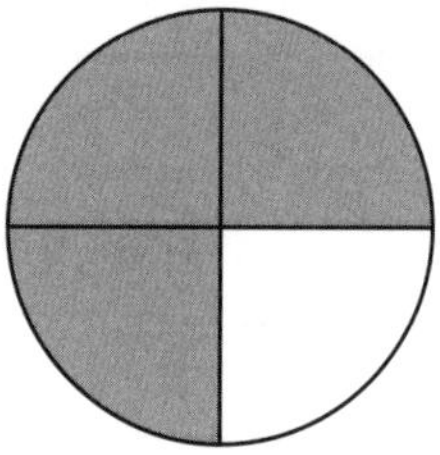

____

8.

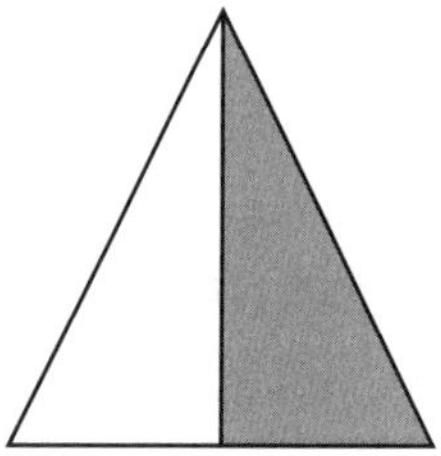

____

Fraction Math

Directions: Add the following fractions.

1. $\frac{2}{5} + \frac{3}{5} =$ ____________

2. $\frac{1}{8} + \frac{4}{8} =$ ____________

3. $\frac{1}{3} + \frac{1}{3} =$ ____________

4. $\frac{2}{6} + \frac{3}{6} =$ ____________

5. $\frac{1}{4} + \frac{3}{4} =$ ____________

6. $\frac{4}{10} + \frac{3}{10} =$ ____________

Directions: Subtract the following fractions.

7. $\frac{4}{8} - \frac{1}{8} =$ ____________

8. $\frac{5}{6} - \frac{2}{6} =$ ____________

9. $\frac{7}{10} - \frac{3}{10} =$ ____________

10. $\frac{3}{4} - \frac{2}{4} =$ ____________

11. $\frac{3}{3} - \frac{2}{3} =$ ____________

12. $\frac{8}{9} - \frac{6}{9} =$ ____________

Directions: Solve the following problems.

13. $\frac{2}{3} + \frac{1}{3} =$ ____________

14. $\frac{2}{6} - \frac{1}{6} =$ ____________

Tally Marks

Directions: Follow the diretions in each box.

1. Use tally marks to show 10.

2. Use tally marks to show 12.

3. Use tally marks to show 9.

4. Count the tally marks.
Write the number below.

5. Count the tally marks.
Write the number below.

Ready·Set·Learn

Rounding

Directions: For each number given, circle the correct rounded number.

1. 48 → 40 or 50?
2. 62 → 60 or 70?
3. 93 → 90 or 100?
4. 15 → 10 or 20?
5. 67 → 60 or 70?
6. 11 → 10 or 20?
7. 19 → 10 or 20?
8. 408 → 400 or 500?
9. 559 → 500 or 600?
10. 232 → 200 or 300?
11. 875 → 800 or 900?
12. 845 → 800 or 900?
13. 341 → 300 or 400?
14. 633 → 600 or 700?
15. 196 → 100 or 200?
16. 255 → 250 or 260?

Problem Solving

Directions: Circle the correct answer in each box.

1. The horse trailer costs $3,076. The horse costs $4,803. What is the total cost for both items?

A. $1,727
B. $1,879
C. $7,879
D. $7,978

2. The newest computer game system regularly costs $5,444. Today it is on sale for $2,331. What is the total savings?

A. $1,331
B. $3,311
C. $7,775
D. $3,113

3. Sybil mixed together $\frac{1}{3}$ cup of vinegar and $\frac{1}{2}$ cup of oil. What is the total amount of liquid ingredients used?

A. 1/5
B. 5/6
C. 2/5
D. 6/5

4. Penny the Party Planner needs 3,123 forks, 3,980 plates, and 1,572 napkins. How many party items does Penny need to get?

A. 8,765
B. 8,567
C. 8,675
D. 7,675

Fun in the Sun

Directions: A survey was taken at Cheatham Middle School to see where the students liked to take their vacations. The pictograph below shows how many students voted for each place. One sun represents 20 votes. Use the pictograph to answer the questions.

Sunny Vacation Spots	
Panama City	
Myrtle Beach	
Gulf Shores	
Virginia Beach	
Cancun	

 = 20 votes

1. Which vacation spot received the most votes? ________________

2. How many students voted for it? ________________

3. Which two vacation spots tied? ________________

4. How many votes did these two receive? ________________

5. Which place received the least number of votes? ________________

6. How many votes did it receive? ________________

7. How many more votes did Gulf Shores receive than Cancun? ______

Tick Tock

Directions: Look at each clock and write the time.

1.

____

2.

____

3.

____

4.

____

5.

____

6.

____

7.

____

8.

____

9.

____

10.

____

11.

____

12.

____

Got the Time?

Directions: Follow the directions in each box.

1. Write this time: one hour before 12:00 P.M.

____

2. Write this time: four hours before 5:00 A.M.

____

3. Write this time: eight hours before 7:00 A.M.

____

4. Solve this problem: School starts at 8:00. Recess is at 10:15. How much time is there between school starting and recess?

______hours ______ minutes

5. Solve this problem: Recess is at 10:15. Lunch is at 12:00. How much time is there between recess and lunch?

______hours ______ minutes

Ways to Measure

Directions: Circle the correct measurement to show how you would measure each item.

1. water in a pool
   a. cup
   b. gallon

2. coffee in a mug
   a. cup
   b. quart

3. lemonade in a pitcher
   a. pint
   b. gallon

4. gasoline in a tank
   a. quart
   b. gallon

5. juice in a glass
   a. cup
   b. quart

6. water in a bathtub
   a. pint
   b. gallon

7. sour cream in a container
   a. pint
   b. gallon

8. oil in an engine
   a. cup
   b. quart

How's the Weather?

Directions: Look at each thermometer. Write the temperature shown.

1. 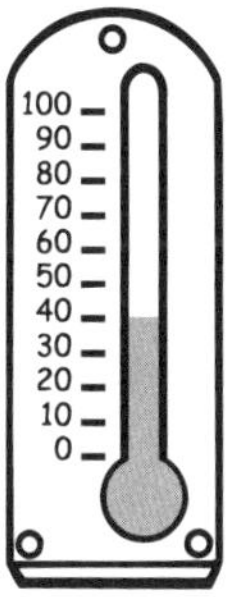

______

2. 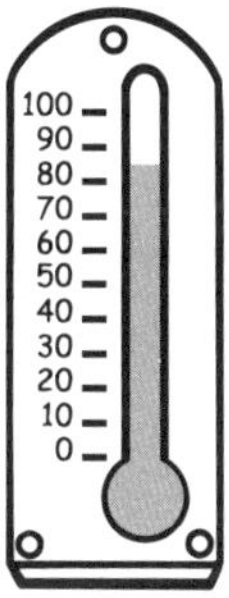

______

3. 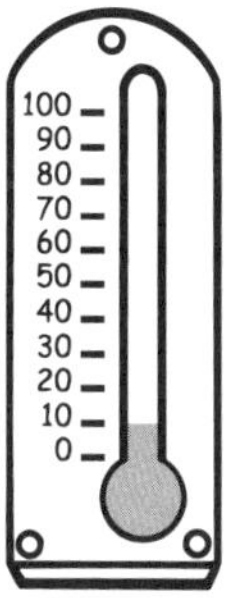

______

4. 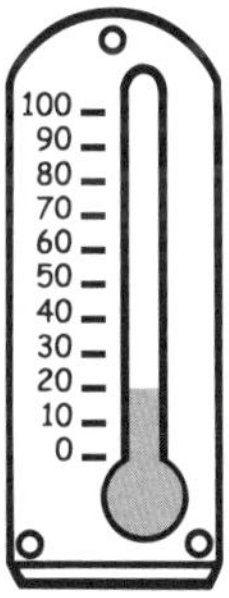

______

5. 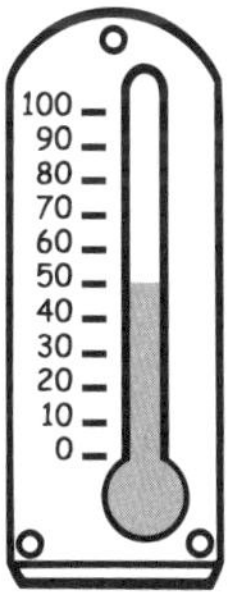

______

6. 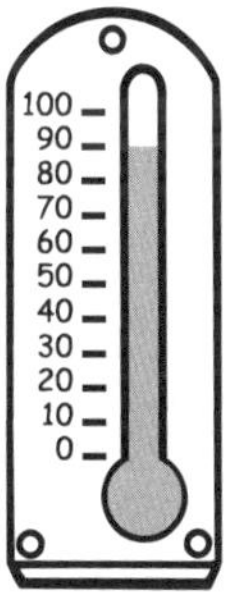

______

Directions: Match each temperature to the correct event.

7. a heavy snow

8. a melting ice cream cone

9. a day when you might need a coat

10. the temperature inside your home

- 98° F
- 55° F
- 70° F
- 30° F

The First Colonies

Directions: Look at the time line and then answer the questions.

1584—British Colonists tried to settle Roanoke near present day North Carolina.

1590—All of the colonists at Roanoke disappeared. It became known as the Lost Colony.

1607—A colony of 105 settlers began the Jamestown settlement in Virginia.

1620—The *Mayflower* left Plymouth England with 102 passengers known as the Pilgrims.

1. In what year was the first successful colony established in America? ______________

2. What happened to the colonists at Roanoke?

____

3. What settlement was founded in 1607? ______________

4. Who arrived on the *Mayflower* in 1620? ______________

Land and Water

Directions: There are seven continents. Can you name them?

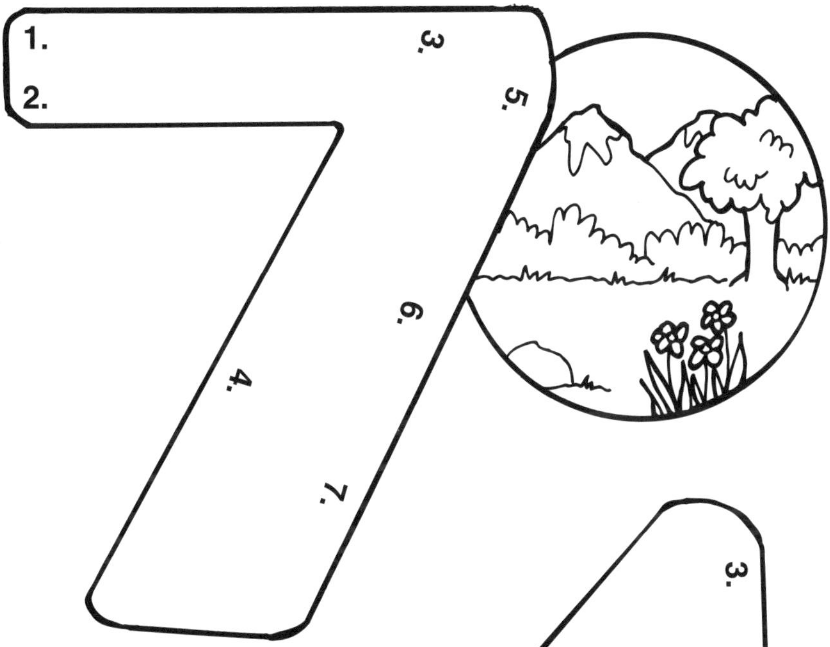

Directions: There are four oceans. Can you name them?

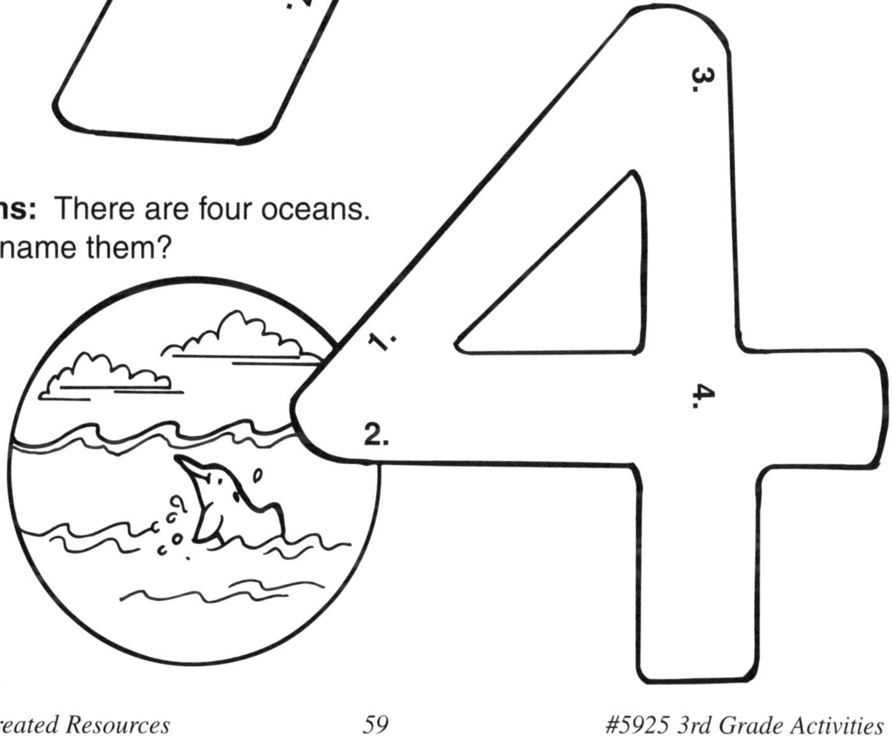

What's Out There?

Directions: Label and color each planet in our solar system. Use the Planet Bank if you need help.

Planet Bank

Mercury	Earth	Jupiter	Uranus
Venus	Mars	Saturn	Neptune

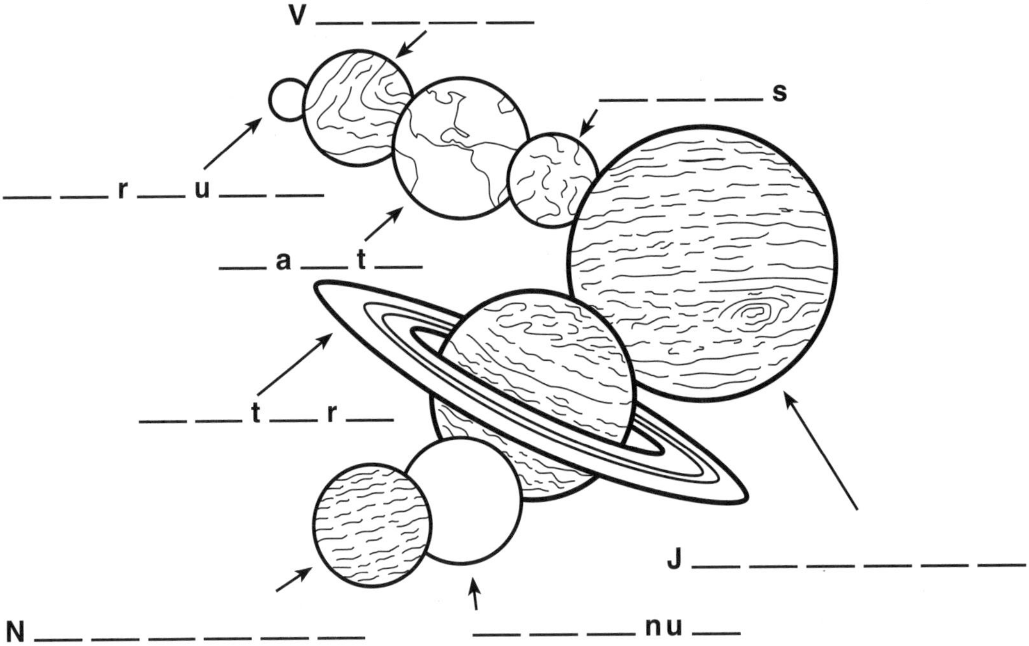

Directions: If you could create a new planet for our solar system, what would you name it? Write your planet's name here.

Answer Key

Page 7
1. pennies
2. ponies
3. berries
4. families
5. factories
6. candies
7. parties
8. cherries
9. babies
10. bellies
11. jellies
12. lilies
13. ladies
14. patties
15. flies
16. stories

Page 8
apples, shirts, coats, movies, stars, cars, trees, computers, flowers, shoes

Page 9
he—Jack
she—Mandy
it—sunshine
we—Joan and I
they—Brett, Sadie, and Phil

Page 10
1. I like to pretend that I can travel through time.
2. Once I pretended to visit a king and queen.
3. They took me to their castle, where I met a dragon.
4. The dragon was friendly, so I named him Norbert.
5. Norbert and I flew around the kingdom in the sky.

Page 11
1. butteros, gauchos, vaqueros
2. A cowboy hat is used to shade the cowboy's eyes from the sun, to keep him dry when it rains, to carry water, and to fan the flames of a campfire.

Page 13
1. enjoys
2. runs
3. marks
4. search
5. splash, leap
6. climb, fall
7. burst
8. wash
9. sit, drink
10. eat, talk

Page 14
1. read
2. watch
3. swims
4. chases
5. climbs
6. run
7. hike
8. count
9. plays
10. fly

Page 15
The present-tense verbs are listed here.
1. finish
2. carry
3. clean
4. paint
5. walk
6. laugh
7. lift
8. grin
9. wrap

Page 16
"The Turtle": slow-moving, hard, many, 475
"The Chameleon": tree-living, sharp, good, long

Page 17
1. d
2. j
3. f
4. g
5. h
6. i
7. c
8. a
9. b
10. e

Page 18
1. .
2. ?
3. !
4. ?
5. .
6. .
7. !
8. .
9. ?
10. ?

Page 19
1. Yes, I would love to go to the movie.
2. We have potato chips, cheese, and chili.
3. Grandma, could we please spend the night?
4. This red car belongs to my mom, and this blue car belongs to my dad.
5. John, may I borrow your football?
6. We saw swans, ducks, and an ostrich.
7. Invite Casey, Jackie, and Toby to go with us.
8. No, we can't go to the zoo today.
9. My sister likes hot dogs, and I like pizza.
10. Aunt Irene, my mom's sister, liked the book, but I liked the movie.

Page 20
1. The bird chased the cat.
2. I wrote a letter to my friend.
3. The family made a puzzle.
4. A penguin jumped into the sea.
5. The puppets sang a song to the audience.

Page 21
Main Idea: Barn owls are fully grown by about 12 weeks of age.

Page 22
Part I: friend, ghost, house, jump, moon, river, silent, tunnel, vest
Part II: cane, cell, deer, dog, lion, loop, lunch, science, sort

Page 23
clockwise, from top left:
3, 2, 4, 5, 1, 6

Page 24
1. quack
2. skin
3. goal
4. swim
5. bird
6. coloring
7. night
8. year
9. winter
10. head

Page 25
Across: 2. hard, 4. back, 6. every, 8. assist, 9. stop
Down: 1. enormous, 3. ancient, 5. abrupt, 7. dim

Page 26
1. I have a dog named Butch who likes to dig, roll, and play fetch.
2. Marvin T. Adams rode his bike to school on September 4, 2007.
3. I like the poem "The Homework Machine" by Shel Silverstein.
4. There is a tall, gnarly tree on Hiss St. in Gainstown, Illinois.
5. While looking out the window, Sheila shouted, "Look out!"

Page 27
9 mistakes: My, jog, night, shoes, Usually, happens, branches, next?, skunk

Page 28
1. C
2. N
3. C
4. C
5. N
6. C
7. N
8. C
9. N
10. C

Page 29
1. "I can't wait for summer vacation," Ted said.
2. "I can't wait, either," Addison agreed.
3. "Where are you going on vacation?" Ted asked.
4. "We're going to Hawaii," Addison said.
5. "That sounds nice," Ted replied.
6. "Where are you going?" Addison asked.
7. Ted replied, "Well, it's not exactly Hawaii, but there is water there."
8. "Well, where is it?" Addison asked again.

Answer Key (cont.)

9. "I'm going to spend my vacation working at my Uncle Bob's carwash," Ted finally told her.
10. "I guess you're right," Addison said with a smile. "There will be plenty of water."

Page 30

1. geese 6. berries
2. stories 7. ladies
3. men 8. deer
4. oxen 9. pennies
5. leaves 10. women

Page 31

Proper Nouns: Jennifer, Fridays, Joe, Mom, Dad, Chloe, Kayla Beth, Ella, Gage, Sally, Tuesday

Common Nouns: pizza, supper, friend, person, cake, game, sisters, bus, students, school, teacher, apple, teacher, pencil, snake, tree, day

Page 33

1. Emily's candy
2. Chien's DVD
3. Tyrese's backpack
4. Rafael's camera
5. Keysha's necklace
6. Elissa's game
7. Sharon's puzzle
8. Samuel's shoes
9. Aina's book
10. Brody's bike

Page 34

4. rabbit
5. kangaroo

Page 35

1. 8, 10, 12, 14, 16, 18, 20, 22, 24, 26
2. 12, 15, 18, 21, 24, 27, 30, 33, 36, 39
3. 16, 20, 24, 28, 32, 36, 40, 44, 48, 52
4. 12, 1, 13, 2, 9
5. 11, 4, 15, 5, 16

Page 36

Across: 1. eighty, 4. ninety, 8. twenty, 9. thirty

Down: 2. hundred, 3. fifty, 4. ten, 5. sixty, 7. forty

Page 37

1. 61 4. 322
2. 492 5. 133
3. 98

In order: 61, 98, 133, 322, 492

Page 38

1. 33 7. 45
2. 55 8. 15
3. 31 9. 10
4. 31 10. 33
5. 58 11. 10
6. 27 12. 45

Page 39

1. 67 7. 48
2. 99 8. 102
3. 111 9. 90
4. 87 10. 114
5. 95 11. 99
6. 110 12. 96

Page 40

1. 214 9. 214
2. 432 10. 355
3. 827 11. 65
4. 440 12. 93
5. 191 13. 73
6. 120 14. 10
7. 362 15. 35
8. 239

Page 41

1. 153.93 5. 85.48
2. 98.88 6. 91.32
3. 78.69 7. $37.77
4. 89.88 8. $13.53

Page 42

1. 16, 16 4. 12, 12
2. 25, 25 5. 16, 16
3. 18, 18 6. 28, 28

Page 45

1. 3 7. 1
2. 2 8. 4
3. 9 9. 11
4. 5 10. 6
5. 7 11. 8
6. 12

You are smart!

Page 46

1. 16¢ 5. 45¢
2. 45¢ 6. 87¢
3. 35¢ 7. 79¢
4. 50¢ 8. 50¢

Page 47

1. 8 4. 5
2. 10 5. 3
3. 5 6. 4

Page 48

1. 1/3 5. 7/10
2. 1/4 6. 2/6
3. 5/6 7. 3/4
4. 3/5 8. 1/2

Page 49

1. 5/5 8. 3/6
2. 5/8 9. 4/10
3. 2/3 10. 1/4
4. 5/6 11. 1/3
5. 4/4 12. 2/9
6. 7/10 13. 3/3
7. 3/8 14. 1/6

Page 50

4. 15 5. 22

Page 51

1. 50 9. 600
2. 60 10. 200
3. 90 11. 900
4. 20 12. 800
5. 70 13. 300
6. 10 14. 600
7. 20 15. 200
8. 400 16. 260

Page 52

1. C 3. B
2. D 4. C

Page 53

1. Panama City
2. 100
3. Myrtle Beach and Virginia Beach
4. 60
5. Cancun
6. 40
7. 40

Page 54

1. 5:15 7. 10:00
2. 9:30 8. 3:30
3. 6:15 9. 4:30
4. 6:30 10. 1:15
5. 11:15 11. 2:30
6. 7:00 12. 3:00

Page 55

1. 11:00 A.M.
2. 1:00 A.M.
3. 11:00 P.M.
4. two hours and 15 minutes
5. one hour and 45 minutes

Page 56

1. b 5. a
2. a 6. b
3. a 7. a
4. b 8. b

Page 57

1. 40° 6. 90°
2. 85° 7. 30°
3. 10° 8. 98°
4. 20° 9. 55°
5. 50° 10. 70°

Page 58

1. 1607
2. They disappeared.
3. Jamestown
4. 102 Pilgrims

Page 59

Continents: Africa, Antarctica, Asia, Australia, Europe, North America, South America

Oceans: Arctic, Atlantic, Indian, Pacific

Page 60

Planets, in order from the sun: Mercury, Venus, Earth, Mars, Jupiter, Saturn, Uranus, Neptune

This Award Is Presented To

____

for

- ★ Doing Your Best
- ★ Trying Hard
- ★ Not Giving Up
- ★ Making a Great Effort